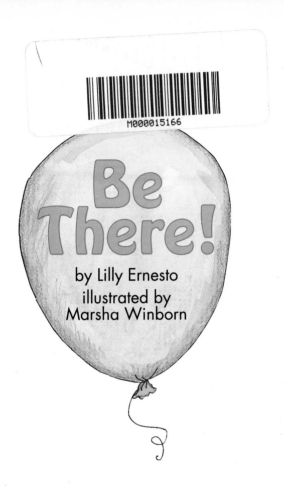

Be There!

by Lilly Ernesto

illustrated by
Marsha Winborn

Scott Foresman

Editorial Offices: Glenview, Illinois • New York, New York
Sales Offices: Reading, Massachusetts • Duluth, Georgia
Glenview, Illinois • Carrollton, Texas • Menlo Park, California

We must be there.
Look at the clock.
It is time to go!

Look at the clock, friend.

It is time, I know.

3

Look at the clock.

It is time for fun!

Look at the clock.
It is time to run!

Look at the clock.
It is time to eat!

Look at the clock.

It is time to be in a seat.

Look at the clock.
It is time for our
pretty, pretty cat.

8

Look at the clock.

It is time to bat.

Look at the clock.
It is time to ride.

Look at the clock.
It is time to slide.

Look at the clock.

Is is time to hop.

Look at the clock.

It is time to stop.

Look at the clock.
It is time for a friend.

Look at the clock.
It is time for . . .

THE END.